MARK TRAIL'S® BOOK OF ANIMALS

(NORTH AMERICAN MAMMALS)

By ED DODD

SCHOLASTIC 

BOOK SERVICES

Published by Scholastic Book Services, a division
of Scholastic Magazines, Inc., New York, N.Y.

 This edition is published by Scholastic Book Services, a division of Scholastic Magazines, Inc., by arrangement with Hawthorn Books, Inc.

6th printing........................November 1968

Printed in the U.S.A.

CONTENTS

MOOSE

The mighty moose, tallest and heaviest deer in the world, is a prized trophy of big game hunters.

Standing
well over
six feet at
the shoulders
and weighing up
to 1800 lbs., the
bull moose carries a
6½ foot spread of antlers.

Because
his legs are so
long and his
neck so short,
he must spread
his forelegs wide
apart in order to
reach low-growing plants.

Though he appears clumsy, he can pass through the dark spruce jungles with the ease and silence of a mouse.

He finds succulent pond lilies irresistible, and consequently spends most of his time up to his neck in water.

With the coming of fall, the bull bellows out his love song and thrashes his huge antlers noisily against the surrounding vegetation . . . Frequent battles for the favors of a homely cow moose end in a death struggle.

When the drifting snows get too deep for his long legs, the moose and his family "yard up."

During these lean months the snow-bound moose strip bark and buds from saplings, often "riding" them down to reach the tender tops.

ELK

Wapiti, the indian name meaning "pale deer," refers to the light-colored winter coat of the elk.

Second only to the moose in size, the stag elk is as big as a horse, and his widely branching rack is an impressive sight . . .

When the first American frontiersmen began the westward push their main source of meat was the elk, for the big deer ranged over the entire continent.

The pale winter coat is so snug and thick that little heat escapes from the wapiti's body, and sub-zero weather causes him little discomfort.

Led by a wise old female who knows the safest route, the elk herds migrate from winter quarters in sheltered valleys to lush meadows high in the mountains.

Until fall the bulls nurse their tender antlers, but with the first frosty days of autumn their musical "bugling" echoes through the hills.

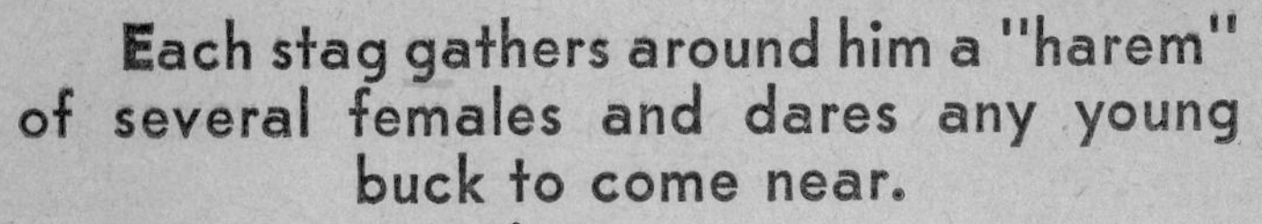

Each stag gathers around him a "harem" of several females and dares any young buck to come near.

But the defensive fighting for protection of calves is left to the females, and the "pile-driver blows" delivered by an infuriated cow put even a bear to flight.

For several days after he is born the spotted calf has no scent, and by lying motionless in the grass he is seldom discovered by predators.

WHITETAIL DEER

With a larger bag of tricks than a sly old fox, the whitetail has more than held his own against guns and predatory enemies.

When man cleared vast wilderness areas and converted them into farmlands, the wily Virginia deer simply added fresh vegetables to his menu and continued to multiply.

The whitetail establishes himself in a wooded area and refuses to leave it, no matter how much he is harried by dogs or hunters.

When surprised he bursts from cover with startling speed and takes off like the wind, but he soon halts and listens for sounds of pursuit.

Often the whitetail eludes dogs by back-tracking and leaping several feet to one side of his trail, where he lies quietly until the confused pack finally passes by.

The crafty doe hides her fawn in the dappled shadows of leafy undergrowth, and when enemies get too near she leads them away on a "wild goose chase."

When the fawn is strong enough to flee from danger, he follows his mother's bobbing white tail through twilight woods as she leads him to safety.

A buck deer's age cannot be determined by the size or number of points on his antlers, for diet and general health control their growth.

The whitetail's antlers usually do not reach trophy size until he is three or four years old, then each year's growth becomes smaller as he approaches old age.

WHITETAIL DEER

PRONGHORN ANTELOPE

The pronghorn holds the distinction of being the only member of his kind on the North American continent.

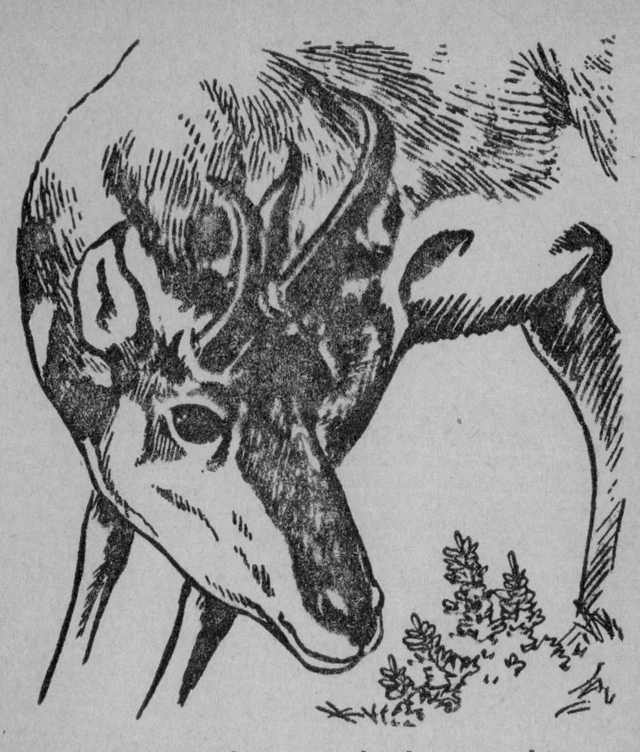

The curious horns, which give this antelope his name, are actually composed of hairs glued together by a strong cementing substance; yet unlike his near relatives, the sheep, goats and oxen, the pronghorn sheds his horns **EACH** year.

Sharp eyesight is more important to the antelope than a sense of smell, for in the open prairies where he lives there is little cover to hide him from enemies.

Coyotes and other predators are seemingly ignored until almost within springing distance; then, with a snort, the graceful prongbuck streaks away at sixty miles an hour . . . leaving all enemies hopelessly behind.

As the
antelope
takes flight he
erects the fluffy
hairs of his rump
patch, and the sun
reflecting on them produces
a brilliant flash of white
alerting other antelope nearby.

The doe antelope is quick to defend her fawn, and she will fight savagely with sharp-edged hooves against coyotes, rattlesnakes and other small enemies.

Larger foes are led away from the odorless, camouflaged fawn by the "lame leg" trick.

PRONGHORN

MOUNTAIN GOAT

High above timberline the
mountain goat blends
perfectly with the
perpetual snowdrifts
of the rugged
windswept peaks.

Actually, the mountain goat is closely related to the pronghorn, for he is an antelope and **NOT A GOAT.**

Most of the predators which dare the steep Alpine slopes to stalk him must approach from below, so the "old man of the mountains" fails to watch the rocks above.

Wise hunters take advantage of this peculiarity by climbing above their quarry and taking him by surprise.

Avalanches and other natural hazards account for the deaths of more mountain goats than well-aimed bullets.

Young kids often fall prey to eagles, but if the mother is near she quickly discourages their attacks with her needle-sharp horns.

Mountain goats climb sheer rock walls, which to the naked eye appear perfectly smooth . . . but the tiniest projection seems to be all "Old Billy" needs for a foothold.

Only the severest winters can drive the mountain goat from his blizzard-swept heights to the protection of the timberline trees.

MOUNTAIN GOAT

AMERICAN BISON

Once as numerous as the nickels which bear his image, the bison ranged from northern Canada to Mexico, and from Pennsylvania and Georgia to the Rocky Mountains.

Before the arrival of white men millions of great shaggy bison covered the landscape as they migrated between winter and summer feeding grounds.

Each year the thundering herds followed the same migration routes, and many of the trails were worn two to three feet deep.

Engineers, laying out railway systems, often utilized these "expressways", which proved to be the easiest grades for track-laying.

To many Indian tribes the "buffalo" (as he is erroneously called) was food, shelter and clothing, and wherever the herds moved the Indian followed.

With the arrival of colonists on the North American continent the bison began to diminish, and the first railroad through the West all but sealed his doom.

Today the bison lives in United States and Canadian national parks, where strict protection has saved him from extinction.

BISON
MUSK-OX

MUSK-OX

Sharing the frozen tundra with the caribou, the musk-ox is a denizen of the cheerless Arctic wastes.

Through the bleak months of Arctic night the woolly musk-oxen wander about in bands numbering from six to a hundred.

Following close on the heels of these tundra vagabonds, huge wolves, like ghostly shadows, wait patiently for a cow or a calf to stray from the herd.

When wolves come within range of their weak eyes, the adult animals quickly form an unbroken circle about the calves, presenting the enemy with a ring of death-dealing horns.

In spite of his bulky appearance, the musk-ox frequently eludes Eskimo hunters by racing up steep icy slopes with surprising speed.

Subsisting on moss pawed from beneath the winter snow, the musk-ox has only a few weeks of summer in which to enjoy the short-lived green vegetation.

BLACK BEAR

The black bear, our most common and widely distributed member of the family, is not always black, but sports a variety of colors.

In the East he is coal black; in the West he is often cinnamon brown; in Alaska he is midnight blue; and in British Columbia he is snowy white.

So varied is the black bear's appetite that he seldom finds food scarce . . .

With powerful paws he unearths roots, ants, grubs, and rodents; or with less effort he gorges himself on berries, nuts, grass, ferns and mushrooms . . . to obtain sweets, such as honey, he'll endure the angry attacks of swarming bees or tear the roof off a locked cabin.

Tree climbing is more often sport than necessity, for he has few enemies he cannot equal in a fair fight . . . normally, however, the black bear leads a carefree, peaceful existence.

Perhaps his solitary life leads the black bear to establish "sign posts"... these bruin "bulletin boards" are carefully read with a keen nose by every passing bear, who then hugs the post or scratches his back against it . . . reaching as high as possible, he then carves his own signature with teeth and claws.

BLACK BEAR

CANADA LYNX

Though the lynx makes no more noise than a falling snowflake, he forgets himself in mating season . . . and his unearthly yowls and caterwauls announce his presence to other members of his family.

In the spring the female brings forth three or four kittens to roam the trail with her until the following winter.

When snows make going difficult, the lynx puts on furry "snowshoes" and travels easily over the deep drifts.

Among the dim shadows cast by the "northern lights" the gray wildcat moves like a phantom until a careless rabbit brings him charging forth in 3-dimensional fury.

So dependent is he upon the snowshoe hare that periodic die-offs of these normally-abundant creatures cause the starvation of many big cats.

However, the lynx is capable of taking larger game, and sometimes downs deer, caribou, mountain sheep, beaver and fox, but he'll settle for any smaller creature he can catch.

LYNX

COUGAR

The cougar roams the rugged "back country" from the Canadian wilderness to the Argentine pampas.

Some
call the big
tawny mountain
lion a coward, but
perhaps he's
smart and has
learned he
can't win against a
high-powered
telescopic rifle
. . . He'll follow
but seldom
attack
humans.

Old-timers love to tell blood-curdling tales of vicious man-eating "painters" that ambush lonely travelers, but few, if any, are the proven cases of unprovoked attack.

However, he shows no respect for man's property as he helps himself to a rancher's livestock . . . and it quite often costs him his scalp!

The baying of the hounds sends the cougar streaking "cross country" . . . finally he "trees" and resignedly awaits his death.

Although he could easily slash the dog pack to ribbons, for some strange reason he seldom bothers to do battle.

COUGAR

TIMBER WOLF

The spine-chilling wail of the big gray wolf still echoes through the forest from the northern border of the U. S. to the Arctic coastline . . .

In some northern areas the wolf carries a price on his head, and hunters have taken to the air to run down their quarry.

In low-flying planes the wolf-hunters easily spot the dark forms moving against winter snows, and chasing the bewildered creatures into the open they pick them off one by one.

Avoiding civilization like a plague, the American wolf has seldom shown a tendency to molest men, although the European variety has been reported to have waylaid unwary travelers.

The cunning wolf is tenacious, and as long as he can find enough wild game and avoid the livestock owner's property, he may continue to hold his own.

Mating for life, the wolf is a devoted husband and father, keeping his family well-supplied with meat and standing watch over the den.

When the cubs are large enough to hunt, the family, sometimes joined by last year's litter, forms the well-known "wolf pack."

With the precision of a well-trained football squad they close in around a fleeing deer and make the tackle, but then their team-work ends as they fight over the carcass!

In the Arctic the wolf attains larger proportions than his "southern cousins" and wears a white coat to match the eternal snows.

COYOTE

To the uninitiated the song of a coyote on a ghostly moonlit prairie sounds like a quartet of howling banshees.

But to the ears of his lifetime mate, the yodeling of the prairie wolf is a sweet melody and perhaps an invitation to join him for a lamb or pork chop dinner.

Hard times have taught the "old man of the plains" to consider as food **ANY** kind of meat he can obtain, whether it be living or dead.

Where there is plenty of natural game, the coyote wisely leaves the farmers' pigs and sheep alone and does a worthwhile job of keeping the rodent population low.

Nor is fruite overlooked as an item of food, for some of the southerners of the coyote family even develop a craving for watermelon.

A pair of coyotes often hunt jack rabbits together, each taking a turn at running the speedy game in a wide circle and dropping out at the starting point as his partner takes over.

Man has fought the coyote
with guns, poison, and traps
for many years, but instead of being driven
from his home territory the clever
coyote has extended his range
into several states east
of the Mississippi and north to
the Alaskan wilderness.

COYOTE

RED FOX

The red fox is probably the most cunning member of the canine family, and many a hound has found himself completely baffled by the criss-crossing, rail-walking, back-tracking wizard of the trails.

Daring to the point of insolence, the red fox seems to enjoy matching wits with the pack, and sometimes he stops to watch the confusion as the dogs try to unravel his trail.

No matter how hard he is pushed, the red fox will keep within the boundaries of his own "stamping grounds," where he knows the terrain like a book.

In February
the male gives up his
carefree bachelorhood to seek
a mate and set up housekeeping.

Occasionally the pair will dig a den, but usually a hollow log or the burrow of a woodchuck can be remodeled to make a suitable home.

Four to nine cubs are born in April, and while the vixen cares for her family her faithful mate brings food to the den's mouth and keeps watch for danger.

Apparently the red fox mates for life, and both parents share in the job of teaching the young to avoid wolves, lynxes, and eagles.

Though he occasionally "borrows" farmers' prize hens, he earns his keep by destroying great numbers of rats and mice.

The silver and cross foxes are color phases of the red fox . . .

RED FOX

GRAY FOX

GRAY FOX

Neither as large nor as cunning as his red cousin, the gray fox offers poor sport for fox hunters and their famous hounds.

Whereas the red fox seems to enjoy matching wits with the dogs, the gray gets panicky and either holes up or climbs a tree.

The only member of his family that climbs trees, the gray fox not only seeks safety among the branches, but also climbs for juicy fruit of wild grapes and persimmons.

Though not as bold as the red fox, the gray-coated canine has made himself at home in every state in the Union, as well as Canada and Alaska.

In a tree trunk den, sometimes several feet above ground, the vixen brings forth her litter of four or five cubs.

In his search for cottontails, rodents, birds, insects and fruit, the gray fox keeps to a small area, staying with the boundaries no matter how hard he is pressed by hunters.

WOLVERINE

For his size the wolverine, or carcajou, is probably the toughest creature that treads the northern trails.

Savage ferocity combined with a mischievous cunning has made the wolverine an object of hate and dread among trappers.

Largest and most formidable member of the weasel family, the carcajou is well-armed with sharp teeth and claws, and possesses an unbelievable strength in his squat stocky body.

Among the Indians and trappers who must match wits with him, the wolverine is believed to be an evil spirit returned to earth in animal form.

And these legends seem almost to be fact, for the diabolical beast regularly raids traplines, destroying the catch and hiding the traps . . . if he finds an opportunity he will completely wreck an unguarded cabin.

Some woodsmen say that even the mighty grizzly and the cougar will give ground before the vicious carcajou.

Meals in the northern forests and tundra are few and far between, so the "glutton," as he is sometimes called, gorges himself with a tremendous amount of meat when he **DOES** find food.

What the selfish wolverine cannot eat he defiles with a skunk-like scent to prevent other four-footed hunters from sharing.

WOLVERINE

BADGER

The flattened, low-slung build of the badger serves him well in his digging habits.

Under the badger's silvery gray mantle a powerful set of muscles drive the long-clawed forefeet as he tunnels swiftly beneath the prairie.

A keen nose helps him locate the burrows of woods rats or gophers, and so rapidly does he sink a shaft that the rodent has little time to escape!

His rodent-destroying habits are beneficial to the rancher and farmer, but the numerous tunnels the badger digs are a serious hazard to livestock, and therefore he is ruthlessly hunted.

Some people accuse the badger of being cowardly, for he wisely dives down in his burrow if danger threatens.

But should he be surprised in the open, the badger proves to be anything **BUT** timid, for he charges man and beast alike, snapping and slashing with teeth and claws!

When the young badgers are old enough to dig their own dinner their parents teach them to catch ground squirrels, prairie dogs, rats and mice.

BADGER

OTTER

The otter is a happy-go-lucky creature who spends his time fishing and frolicking about his native streams.

Steep banks with smooth clay or snow surfaces make perfect chutes for a sliding game, and hour after hour the otter will climb to the top and **ZIP** down the slippery surface into the water.

On land the otter is rather slow and awkward, but in the water he is graceful and swift, easily overtaking his finny prey.

Winter ice and snow often force the otter to travel over land in search of open water, and he progresses by alternately leaping and sliding on his chest.

Fat beaver kits sometimes prove to be too much of a temptation for the otter, and then a **BATTLE ROYAL** between the otter and members of the beaver colony often results.

Young otters are born in stream-bank dens and stay with the mother until grown.

The female has been known to take her little ones into the water on her back when giving them their first swimming lesson.

OTTER

RACCOON

The "little brother to the bear," as the crafty raccoon is sometimes called, wears the black mask of a bandit.

When he
raids the chicken
house and the farmer's
hound goes after him,
the ring-tailed trickster may
lead him to water.

And should the hound be
foolish enough to jump in
after him, the 'coon
may climb on "old
Bowser's" head
and give him
the dunking
of his life.

In pioneer days coon-skin caps were the fashion, and the raccoon was constantly fleeing for his life.

The human-like footprints left by the raccoon as he searches the shallows for frogs, mussels and crayfish are sometimes mistaken for those of a small child.

When opening clam shells the raccoon is a past master, for his deft fingers quickly find the weakest part and pry it open, and he need never so much as glance at the shell while he works!

The raccoon has an odd habit of washing everything he eats whenever water is available, though his reasons are still his own secret.

The raccoon usually takes to the trees to escape the hounds, but if he finds himself cornered he faces his tormentors and puts up a stiff battle.

RACCOON

BEAVER

The remarkable engineering skill of the beaver seems to go beyond mere instinct as he varies his construction work to meet the requirements of each new building site.

A sturdy dam of mud and sticks holds back the water to form a moat around the beaver's house.

The single room of the beaver bungalow is a cozy, smooth-floored chamber a few inches above water level, and roofed over with hard-packed mud.

If the house is threatened by predators, several exits with underwater openings permit the beaver to leave unnoticed.

With the approach of the mating season the male beaver makes mud pies perfumed with his own special scent and leaves them in prominent places to attract his lady friend.

All summer the beavers cut and haul green sticks to the pond-bottom storage pile, and when ice covers the surface of the water they have plenty of tender bark to keep them fat and healthy.

With bright orange teeth, he cuts down aspen, willow, and birch for food and dam building.

With his broad flat tail the beaver slaps the water to warn other members of the colony that man, wolf, or lynx is on the prowl . . .

BEAVER

INDEX